When Pain Knocks At Your Door

Lourdes Salazar

When Pain Knocks At Your Door

A Testimony Of Hope For The Loss Processes

All Rights Reserved © 2024 by Lourdes Salazar

ISBN: 979-8-89412-145-1

Editing & Designs: Benny Rodríguez (AcademiaDeAutores.com)

Category: Christian Living / Grief

Contents

Dedication

I dedicate this book, first, to the Father, Son and, Holy Spirit.

To my son Nelson "*Toño*" Colón and my sister in Christ, whom I love very much.

To Sister Moreno who always motivated me to write and always believed in this book and me even when I didn't believe it. Although you are no longer with us, you are in my heart and will always be there. Thank you!

To Pastor Vicky Aquino, for being there with me. Thank you to my church, who are a light on the path.

But most of all, I thank my children: Job, Ángel and Juan Martínez. If I were born again, I would ask the Lord for you to be my children. I love them.

To my granddaughters and my grandson, who I love with my heart.

To Tina, Tito, Teresa, and everyone I can't name, but you know who they are.

Thanks to my sister who raised me, Minerva, Sonia and all my family and friends. Thank you for pushing me violently. God bless you very much.

Thanks to my favorite prophet...he knows who he is. I love you all.

Foreword

Dr. Vicky Santiago de Aquino

This book, "*When Pain Knocks at Your Door*," talks about the process of loss, which is always painful. This causes many changes in the family members.

And the battle begins. It is a process of accepting the reality of loss. The pain of grief is experienced and forces us to adapt to life without the person's physical presence. It's easy to lose your reason for living. Each person experiences grief differently. This means that there are periods of intense, painful feelings that come and go. People may feel like they are making progress in grieving when they temporarily feel less pain. But after a while, they can grieve again.

Such changes in grief can occur on important dates, such as holidays or birthdays. Over time, some people experience these grief cycles less frequently as they adjust to the loss.

But in this book, you will receive strength, which you need to get back up. The Holy Spirit has directed Pastor Lourdes to write so that through these written lines you receive the message that will bless your life, and you will find that medicine for your heart.

"Let us then approach God's throne of grace with confidence, so that we may receive mercy and find grace to help us in our time of need." (Hebrews 4:16)

"Cast all your anxiety on him because he cares for you." (1 Peter 5:7)

"Jesus said to her, "I am the resurrection and the life. The one who believes in me will live, even though they die; **26** *and whoever lives by believing in me will never die. Do you believe this?"*(John 11:25-26)

Do you believe it with me?

Introduction

Writing this book was not easy, because it is reliving what has already happened. However, in the time that has passed, I have seen so many people lose loved ones. I have also seen how depression and sadness have tried to stop them because they do not know where to go. I would like you, through this book, to find that Peace that only the Lord can give us through His Love, through that very special Presence of the Almighty God.

The psalmist says: *"For one day in their courts is better than a thousand outside of them."* I would like people who have lost loved ones to know that we hope to see them again one day. How do I know? Because it is what the Lord has promised us, and it is what I believe.

The word does not lie. Our thoughts are not like those of the Lord, because He only thinks of good and not evil. Logically, that there are things that I will never understand about the Lord, but if He decides it, He also knows what is best for us.

I know my son is in a better place. God has given me the Peace that I needed, and I would like you, my dear reader, to also be able to put your trust in the Lord. I know that at the moment we can feel that our soul is also failing along with that being. At a time like this, just remember what Psalm 16: 10 and 11 says:

"Because you will not abandon me to the realm of the dead, nor will you let your faithful one see decay. You make known to me the path of life; you will fill me with joy in your presence, with eternal pleasures at your right ha nd."

I want to tell you that God is always with us. That we are not alone, because He is our strength, our strong castle. He is the Almighty, the King of Kings, the Lord of Lords, He is our everything.

When Pain Knocks
At Your Door

T his is a topic I thought I would never talk about. It all started on October 5, 2019, when Toño started to feel bad. At the time, he lived in Bronx, NY. Suddenly, he had to take a detour and go to the hospital.

There he had had a stroke. That Sunday, she left for church happy, as usual. Arriving at the church, I began to feel very sad and as I passed through the church door I couldn't explain why I felt so much pain. Immediately, I began to pray and told the Lord: *"Something is happening to Toño, I can feel i t."*

Suddenly, Evelyn enters through the church door and tells me: *"Pastor, I was very happy, and when I got here to the church parking lot I started to feel very sad that I can't explain."* Thus, I continued the entire service with my heart desperate because I called Toño several times, and he did not answer me.

So, I went with my friend Williams to Joisy's house. Curiously, my son Toño's partner called me three times, but she didn't talk to me at all. My oldest son, Juan, asked her not to tell me on the phone that her son, Toño, was in a coma. I insisted and called again and no one answered me. I told Joisy and Williams: *"Something's up with Toño, I know it."*

Around 9pm, my youngest son finally called me. I immediately told her: *"I have such great sadness in my heart and I know that something is happening, but I don't know what it is."* With a warm voice, Juan told me: *"Pray, mommy, pray until you fall asleep."* At around 1:30am, Juan called and ask me what I was doing. I responded: *"Crying... I don't know what's happening, but my heart is sad, and I don't know why."*

The first thing that didn't give me peace was that my son never calls me at that time to ask me what I was doing. In the call, he told me, *"Come outside, I'm here."* That's when I got even more nervous. When I opened the door, I didn't look at him and just looked in the direction of his car. I asked him, *"Where are Anabel and Alanis?"* I know he doesn't go out without his family. Juan only told me: *"I'm here for another reason. Look for a little bundle of clothes because we have to go to NY. Toño is in the hospital but calm."*

The shock was so great that I had to go to the emergency room, and he spoke to the doctors so they could inject me with some medicine and calm me down. Afterward, I went to church and left the church card with Williams under my bible in the office, and we continued our trip to NY.

Facing the Situation

I t was on October 6 in the hospital parking lot that I told Juan: "*Well, here you are going to tell me what I am going to face. I can't face something I don't know. Tell me here and now.*" Juan told me with his head down: "*Toño is intubated and in a coma.*" I drew strength from where I didn't have it and told him, "*Ok, let's go.*" I can tell you that it was there where for the first time I told the Lord "*Help me because I won't be able to do it alone.*" As the word says, "*Let the weak say, I am strong.*"

I needed all the strength that only the God of Heaven could give me. These are the moments where the only thing that can help us are the words treasured in our hearts that God has given us. It was a very strong impression when I saw him in bed. I felt like the world had collapsed on me, but even so, the Lord gave me the strength and I said: *"Do you hear me... it's me, and you arrived in the ambulance, but we left here together."* He shed tears because I think that when he saw me, he was filled with hope. He never saw me cry, not because he wouldn't cry, but because I didn't cry in front of him.

But I felt like my world was collapsing, and I started doing what I knew I had to do: pray, pray, pray. Cry out to the only true God, the only one who could help me. That's why I decided to write my story asking God in heaven to help someone who has lost a loved one, in the same way he helped me. It is with the help of the Lord that we can go through these strong and difficult moments in our lives. Only God gives us the strength and peace we need.

We continued like this for days, watching how, little by little, with the help of the Lord and the doctors, we went through the hard process. It was not easy to see with so many tubes and cables.

I also saw my cousin suffer, and she was there all the time until the last day. He had asked everyone to pray for him. Every day, she repeated to myself: *"Let the weak say, I am strong."*

These are moments where if you are not firmly attached to the Lord, I don't know how you would do it. It really is spent, one day at a time, trusting in the will of the Lord.

Little by little, we began to see how he recovered, but he still could not speak well or move his entire left side. Watching that scene, I had to stop for a while, because my breathing felt very strong and my chest and back hurt.

I went to eat something, took the train back to my aunt and sister's house to take a bath, and later I returned to the hospital. All of Toño's communication was signs since he still couldn't speak. Even before that picture, my hopes were firm, because my faith was placed in the Creator. Everything he had preached during my life, he was now reminding me.

I liked sleeping in the hospital. I didn't want to leave because I felt that if he left, I would lose him. It was so hard to see my family so sad, especially my son Juan.

To console him, I acted *"strong"* but the truth is that I was broken. I told myself that when we leave here, I'm going to pick up all my little pieces, and I'm going to make myself new because God still hadn't told me the end.

He was someone so loving. He understood everything, he looked for the positive side of life in everything. He was a warrior, a true warrior.

The Third Day

Every day they bathed him and changed his clothes in bed. The scene is not easy for a mother. To make matters worse, her blood began to clot, and the doctors didn't know why. His condition worsened immediately, and they ordered me to be taken out of the room. Nobody could explain the reason to me. When everything returned to normal, I returned to pray next to him.

I learned one thing from him when we were in the church where we congregated. He prayed in the living room of our apartment for 4 and 5 hours, and I witnessed how his prayers were answered. I still remember how he and Obi prayed in the room, saying: *"Let's see the victory that the Lord will give us."*

Those same words were what I was now saying in his ear. When he went into a medical crisis, he looked at me because he didn't want me to be scared. Although I was praying, I felt that I was the one leaving along with him. Only someone who has been through this can understand.

The days were endless, and we kept praying for a miracle. Several days later, the tube he had in his mouth was removed. Holy God! How much joy it brought to my heart, but even so he couldn't speak, and what he was saying couldn't be understood.

Nurses came and went, doing blood tests and giving shots in his belly. The saddest thing was when the doctor there said that he had to operate on the vessel, which caused his health to decline again. Meanwhile, I kept asking everyone to continue praying. I want to pause here because I want to thank Desiré and his family (they called me every day) and Tina, who wanted to go with me to the hospital. Although his intentions were noble, I told them that they couldn't because they didn't want us to stay in the room.

Shortly after, Toño was brought in from the operating room. His look was sad. The support of my family in those moments was key. I appreciate it! They never left me alone at any time. To the people who worked with him, I always told them that he was someone very special, not because he was my son, but because since he was born he was beautiful.

He had a big and humble heart. He was a good brother, son, friend, and partner, and I am sure he was a great father. Nobody knows what a mother suffers when she sees a child in the hospital. He just cried and cried, especially when no one was there. Only an older lady from India heard me cry, and she ran her hand over my head. She told me: "*He is strong, but pray keep praying, don't stop praying.*"

Incredible Moments

S o the days continued to pass and they took away the breathing machine. They left him alone with oxygen since he could breathe on his own now. Just when I thought everything was calming down, another *"storm"* came. They had to have emergency surgery for the second time because he was bleeding internally.

When they operated on the vessel, it seemed that they lacerated his stomach and that's why he kept making signs because it caused him a lot of pain. In this new surgery, they had to cut part of his stomach. The wait was very sad. I knew he was suffering and I couldn't do anything.

I could only pray and tell myself: *"I can do all things through Christ who strengthens me."* In those moments, I remembered the day we accepted the Lord together. He remembered everything we had laughed about. He tried to hide my pain with stories since he had no other way to console me. I whispered in his ear: *"Calm down, this is going to happen."*

How sad it was when he looked at me without being able to speak well. I had to give him words of encouragement when I felt like I was the one dying. I also saw how he smiled at me so as not to see my sadness. That was even stronger for me.

The time came when they were going to change his room, but they no longer allowed anyone to stay, including me. His 39th birthday was approaching, and we wanted to celebrate it in some way. Finally, October 31, 2019, the day of his birth, arrived and everything was very nice. His daughters, his friends, Ivette, Víctor, co-workers, family, and me came. That night, his partner brought him the Carvel cake he wanted. He was so happy.

It was also the night that, upon arriving at Minerva's house, the Lord showed it to me in a box for the first time while I was looking at some photos. You can't imagine how much I cried that night. I asked the Lord again and again to leave it with me a little longer.

I surrendered to God once again and told him: *"If you don't help me, I won't be able to... please help me."* The next day, he told me to look for a big house in Florida or Connecticut because he wanted to go with me and leave NY. He was very tired and too stressed. I only answered *"Yes"*, that he would look for the house, but that I was sure the house was there. He wanted to have peace, and he didn't know God's plan. How sad when you can't do anything! All you have to do is place yourself in God's hands and ask him not to let you go.

The Final Thrust

As best we could, we celebrated his 39 years and his entire family, daughters, and friends were there. I have to tell you, not because he was my son, but he was very loved by all the people who knew him.

It was a special and beautiful night for him. For me, it was the saddest because it was the night that the Lord showed him to me in the coffin and even today writing this book, you don't know how much it hurts me.

God's faithfulness has been with me all the time. I learned that there are processes that we go through with people supporting us, but there are other deserts that need to be crossed alone. Without anyone who understands you more than the Lord or someone who has been through the same thing.

I imagined Jairus being told not to bother the Master anymore because his daughter had died! What strong words, but how good that the Lord ended up visiting Jairus' house. It wasn't that he couldn't do something for me. He made me understand that it was better the way He had decided.

It's not easy to say "*NO*" to our parents when they ask us for something. So, how do I say no to the one who gave me life and gave me the privilege of being his mother? How can you tell him, not to do it when He has already decided to take him? I could only say to Him: "*Leave it to me a little longer, please*" and I think He left it to me for an extra 15 days.

The days that followed were agony. After his stroke, he had three operations in one month, and we still didn't know the cause of his clots. His divine strength, operating in us through our faith, was the key. His word says that we can do all things through Christ, who strengthens us.

The Price Of His Glory

"For our light and momentary troubles are achieving for us an eternal glory that far outweighs them all." (2 Corinthians 4:17)

T he human being thinks that the momentary tribulation will pass quickly. But, as time continues to pass, birthdays, Christmases, and many other things arrive, you collide with the reality that that loved one is really gone and will not return. That is when we have to hold onto the mantle of the Lord, his hand, and not let go. That's when we quote the Word to the Lord in prayer and all you can hear is *"Everything is going to be okay."*

In moments like this, we want to exchange our lives for the ones we loved so much. We have to totally trust in the GREAT I AM. They were moments of praying under intense pain of anguish. While he wrote to everyone to continue praying, he also asked the Lord for forgiveness and every day he asked for mercy from him. He desperately wanted my God to change his mind and regret taking me. He had already told me, and I know that He is not a bad God. Deep down inside, I knew why He allowed me to go through something so hard.

He does not give us burdens that we cannot carry. There are times when we have to understand that only with the Lord can we get through these difficult times. Today I am certain that he is with the Lord and that comforts me. I know that one day we will see each other again. The day of our farewell was approaching. I didn't know it, but I knew it would happen. The decision has been made and no matter how much I cried, nothing was going to change. Only His peace, which surpasses any understanding, could attend to my pain.

The Day Has Arrived!

November 15, 2019

U nfortunately, my son's time on earth had come to an end. It was 6 am when Obi arrived at my sister's apartment and told me: *"Get dressed, we have to go to the hospital."* I did not know what to do. I turned from here to there and from there to here. I couldn't hold it in anymore until I turned around and told him: *"You came to tell me that Toño died."*

Without being able to do anything, he began to cry like a little child because he loved his brother. How sad was my day! But in his infinite mercy, the Lord had already shown it to me, so I was able to prepare a little more, it was not easy.

How difficult it is for a mother to lose a child! Especially if he is so attached to you. When I saw him in that motionless hospital bed, he looked like he was 16 years old again. The impact was so hard that they had to leave me in the hospital for 5 days. He told everyone who came into the room: *"My baby died."*

I thought about how our Father in heaven would feel when his daughter died for us. How much suffering he had for us to be saved. How much pain to just give us back the authority that we lost in the Garden of Eden? How sad that many, today, cannot value his sacrifice. For many, it cost nothing, but it cost Him everything.

The Final Day

November 21, 2019

I know it wasn't goodbye but see you later. I opened my eyes to the reality of pain that my son was no longer in the land of the living. I had to face everything hard, but I thank Jesus Christ and all those who were with me, family, pastors, brothers in faith, and the church who were present.

I want to extend special gratitude to my three spiritual children who were with me. I didn't put their names because they know who they are. And to the one who was looking out for me all the time, I have no more words to say, thank you! You know who you are! Faced with such a moving scene, in my mind I thought: *"A little angel with green eyes escaped and went to meet his King."*

That was the last night I saw him, and I would give everything to see him again. I have the consolation that one day we will see us again, and I will be able to hug him, kiss him like the first day I had him in my arms.

I thank the Lord for being my strength, my strong castle. Without Him, I would never have made it. Being able to get here, only with Jesus.

Surrender and Weeping

November 23, 2019

That Saturday morning, I gave it to him. Needless to say, I cried, cried, and cried like never before. Now I had to leave New York to return to the *"Land of Lodebar."* I had to return to my hometown of Ocala, where I would begin the next phase of learning to deal with the pain of accepting the unacceptable. To accept the will of the Lord and tell him how you want. They were horrible days, full of anxiety and pain, a lot of pain.

Having been strengthened by the Lord, I am now prepared, after almost 3 and a half years, to sit down and write this short testimony. It took me a while to get it done because it's not sweet to have to re-experience the whole story. Still, I know that these simple words can help others find strength in the only source that never fails.

To rest in the only arms that won't let you fall. To experience the peace that surpasses any logic or idea... that which comes from Him. In those moments of despair and many questions, my Father only told me: *"Don't worry, I am with you... and I breathed the breath of life on you."*

Conclusions

And I lived again... Very soon I will continue telling you how the Lord took me out of Lodebar, from the land of my sadness and pain. In his process, he breathed the breath of life upon me, lifted me, prepared me, dressed me again in new clothes, and invited me to dine at his table.

God bless you richly and thank you for taking the time to read "*When Pain Knocks at Your Door.*"

Blessings,

- *Lourdes*

"I can do all things through Christ who strengthens me."

Through The Streets Of Gold And The Sea Of Glass

Special Words

Through the streets of gold and the sea of glass, Mami, Inés, María, and Toño walk. They are singing Jerusalem, how beautiful you are, streets of gold and sea of glass and on the way they meet Luisito and Edwin, and they also join in walking, they continue singing.

Everyone suddenly met Wilfredo and daddy. They met, and he said, *"I want to worship too."* Luisito played the congas, Mami and Tío Junior started singing, and my mother Carmen with the maracas.

Toño said: *"The best worship group was formed"* and Inés told her niece: *"Praise you too so that you feel what I feel, those rivers of living water in your soul and heart."*

Hallelujah! Suddenly someone asked, do you want to go back? And they were all heard in one voice: *"No, no, we do not want to return, here there is no pain or sadness, there is no bitterness or tribulation, only joy, praise and adoration and with the Lord whom we do not want to l eave."*

Thus, all together they continued walking through the New Jerusalem, singing to the Lord all together with a new heart. I'm going to Canaan on my way, I'm going to Canaan on my way...

Pastor Lourdes Salazar

About the Author

Pastor Lourdes Salazar

He was born on February 22, 1959, in Puerto Rico. Since she received Christ, she has been a servant and worshiper of the Lord. She has a Bachelor's Degree in Psychology and a Master's Degree in Pastoral Counseling. She is certified as a Chaplain. God worked miraculously on her to heal her from cancer. She is a faithful believer in the power of God and His Love. She Pastors the church *"Una Luz En El Camino"* in the city of Ocala, Florida.

Memories...

We Will Always Remember You!

Made in the USA
Columbia, SC
25 May 2024

36174269R10026